WHO EATS WHAT?
OUTBACK FOOD CHAINS

by Rebecca Pettiford

pogo

Ideas for Parents and Teachers

Pogo Books let children practice reading informational text while introducing them to nonfiction features such as headings, labels, sidebars, maps, and diagrams, as well as a table of contents, glossary, and index.

Carefully leveled text with a strong photo match offers early fluent readers the support they need to succeed.

Before Reading

- "Walk" through the book and point out the various nonfiction features. Ask the student what purpose each feature serves.
- Look at the glossary together. Read and discuss the words.

Read the Book

- Have the child read the book independently.
- Invite him or her to list questions that arise from reading.

After Reading

- Discuss the child's questions. Talk about how he or she might find answers to those questions.
- Prompt the child to think more. Ask: What other outback animals and plants do you know about? What food chains do you think they are a part of?

Pogo Books are published by Jump!
5357 Penn Avenue South
Minneapolis, MN 55419
www.jumplibrary.com

Copyright © 2017 Jump!
International copyright reserved in all countries. No part of this book may be reproduced in any form without written permission from the publisher.

Library of Congress Cataloging-in-Publication Data

Names: Pettiford, Rebecca, author.
Pettiford, Rebecca. Who eats what?
Title: Outback food chains / by Rebecca Pettiford.
Description: Minneapolis, MN: Jump! Inc. [2016]
Series: Who eats what? | Audience: Ages 7-10.
Includes bibliographical references and index.
Identifiers: LCCN 2016034375 (print)
LCCN 2016034758 (ebook)
ISBN 9781620315774 (hardcover: alk. paper)
ISBN 9781620316160 (pbk.)
ISBN 9781624965258 (ebook)
Subjects: LCSH: Food chains (Ecology)–Australia–Central Australia–Juvenile literature.
Central Australia–Ecology–Juvenile literature.
Australia–Ecology–Juvenile literature.
Classification: LCC QH197 .P48 2016 (print)
LCC QH197 (ebook) | DDC 577.160942–dc23
LC record available at https://lccn.loc.gov/2016034375

Editor: Jenny Fretland VanVoorst
Book Designer: Michelle Sonnek
Photo Researcher: Michelle Sonnek

Photo Credits: Animals Animals, 12-13; Dreamstime, 20-21bm; Getty, cover, 5, 14-15, 20-21t; iStock, 11, 23; Minden, 19; National Geographic, 18; Shutterstock, 1, 3, 4, 10, 16-17, 18, 20-21tm; SuperStock, 6-7, 8-9, 20-21b.

Printed in the United States of America at Corporate Graphics in North Mankato, Minnesota.

TABLE OF CONTENTS

CHAPTER 1

EXPLORING THE OUTBACK

The outback is a **biome** unique to **Australia**. It covers 2.5 million square miles (6.5 million square kilometers) of desert.

During the day, it is hot.

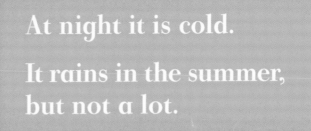

At night it is cold.

It rains in the summer, but not a lot.

In the outback, plants have small leaves. This helps them save water. Boab trees store water in their thick trunks. Some grasses are sharp. This protects the grass from hungry animals.

boab tree ·····▶

WHERE IS IT?

The Australian outback includes deserts throughout the continent.

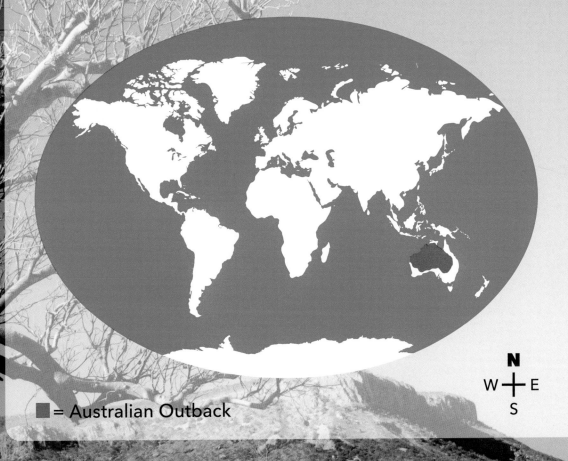

■ = Australian Outback

N
W + E
S

Many animals live in the outback. Some of them are strange. Many are rare. In fact, you can find many animals here that you will not find anywhere else!

DID YOU KNOW?

The outback is a harsh place. Few people live there. Australia's most familiar animals cannot live there, either. For example, koalas and **wombats** live mostly along the coast. So do **wallabies**.

CHAPTER 2

THE OUTBACK FOOD CHAIN

Like all living things, outback plants and animals need energy to grow and move. Food is energy. Plants make their own food. Animals eat plants. They also eat other animals.

A **food chain** shows how energy moves from plants to animals. Each living link in the chain gets energy from the one before it.

In the outback, trees, shrubs, and grasses are **producers**. They use energy from the sun, soil, and water to make food. They are the first link in the food chain.

Kangaroos and **emus** eat plants. So do crickets. They are **consumers**, the next link in the chain.

DID YOU KNOW?

The **bilby** is an outback **omnivore**. It eats plants. But it also eats small animals. It is associated with Easter in Australia. Instead of chocolate rabbits, shops offer chocolate bilbies!

emu
(consumer)

grass
(producer)

dingo
(predator)

Animals such as **dingoes**, **goannas**, and birds of **prey** are **predators**. They hunt and eat consumers. They are the next link in the food chain.

Large predators will eat smaller predators. For example, a saltwater crocodile will eat a dingo.

DID YOU KNOW?

Saltwater crocodiles are the largest **reptiles** in the world. They eat fish, wild pigs, and other animals.

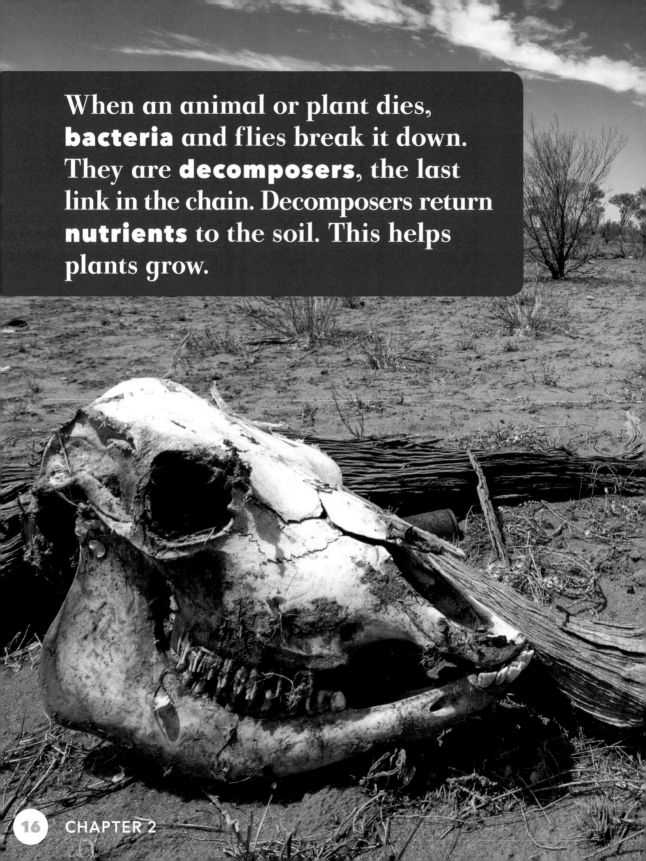

When an animal or plant dies, **bacteria** and flies break it down. They are **decomposers**, the last link in the chain. Decomposers return **nutrients** to the soil. This helps plants grow.

TAKE A LOOK!

One outback food chain might look something like this:

Producer:
Grasses (Seeds)

Predator:
Wedge-tailed Eagle

Consumer:
Parakeet

Decomposer:
Bacteria

CHAPTER 3

FOOD CHAIN CLOSE-UPS

Let's look at a simple food chain. It starts with a fallen fig. A bilby eats it.

A python eats the bilby. In time, the python dies. Bacteria break down its body. The nutrients help plants grow. The food chain continues!

Let's look at another food chain.

1) This one starts with a shrub.

2) A bearded dragon eats its leaves.

3) A dingo eats the dragon.

4) When the dingo dies, flies break down its body.

The nutrients make the soil rich. The food chain begins again!

ACTIVITIES & TOOLS

BREAKFAST FOOD CHAIN

You don't live in the distant outback, but no matter where you live or what you eat, you are part of many food chains. Let's look at a few of them.

Think about what you had for breakfast. Try working backwards to create a food chain for your meal. Did you have eggs? Trace the eggs back to the chicken, the chicken back to the grain, and the grain back to the sun. Did you have milk in your oatmeal? Trace the milk back to the cow, the cow back to the grass, and so on.

Draw a picture of your meal showing the different food chains that combined to create it. See if you can connect the various food chains. For example, the sun made the grass grow. Cows ate the grass and eventually gave you milk. But that same sun grew the grains that made your oatmeal or that fed the chickens that laid the eggs you ate. It grew the trees that gave oranges for your orange juice. How many chains connected to your breakfast did you make?

Australia: A continent in the eastern hemisphere that is southeast of Asia.

bacteria: Tiny life forms that break down dead animals.

bilby: A small, pouched mammal with large ears and soft, gray fur that is active at night and lives in the Australian outback.

biome: A large area on Earth defined by its weather, land, and the type of plants and animals that live there.

consumers: Animals that eat plants.

decomposers: Life forms that break down dead matter.

dingoes: Wild dogs unique to Australia and believed to be descended from semi-domesticated animals.

emus: Large, flightless birds similar to the ostrich.

food chain: An ordering of plants and animals in which each uses or eats the one before it for energy.

goannas: Carnivorous monitor lizards found throughout Australia.

nutrients: Substances that plants and animals need to live and grow.

omnivores: Animals that eat both plants and other animals.

predators: Animals that hunt and eat other animals.

prey: An animal that is hunted or killed by another animal for food.

producers: Plants that make their own food from the sun.

reptiles: Animals that are cold-blooded and have scales and a backbone; most reptiles lay eggs.

wallabies: Australian pouched mammals similar to a small kangaroo.

wombats: Stocky, burrowing, pouched mammals that resemble small bears.

INDEX

TO LEARN MORE

Learning more is as easy as 1, 2, 3.

1) Go to www.factsurfer.com
2) Enter "outbackfoodchains" into the search box.
3) Click the "Surf" button to see a list of websites.

With factsurfer, finding more information is just a click away.